D0174775

Georgia

by the Capstone Press
Geography Department

Reading Consultant:
Nanette McGee
Georgia Department of Education

CAPSTONE PRESS
MANKATO, MINNESOTA

C A P S T O N E   P R E S S
818 North Willow Street • Mankato, Minnesota 56001

Printed in the United States of America.

Library of Congress Cataloging-in-Publication Data
    Georgia/by the Capstone Press Geography Department.
    p. cm.--(One Nation)
    Includes bibliographical references and index.
    Summary: Gives an overview of the state of Georgia, including
    its history, geography, people, and living conditions.
    ISBN 1-56065-473-2
    1. Georgia--Juvenile literature. [1. Georgia.]
    I. Capstone Press. Geography Dept. II. Series.
F286.3.G458 1997
975.8--dc20

                                        96-35116
                                          CIP
                                          AC

Photo credits
Georgia Department of Industry, Trade & Tourism, cover
Flag Research Center, 4 (left)
Unicorn/Ted Rose, 4 (right); Ann Trulove, 5 (left);
    Alice Prescott, 5 (right)
FPG, 26; Peter Gridley, 6, 32; James Blank, 8; E. Alan
    McGee, 16; James Randklev, 21; Ron Thomas, 28
Cheryl Blair, 10
Gary Alan Nelson, 12, 34
Visuals Unlimited/Max and Bea Hunn, 18
James P. Rowan, 22, 25, 30

Table of Contents

Fast Facts about Georgia 4

Chapter 1 News Around the Clock 7

Chapter 2 The Land 11

Chapter 3 The People 17

Chapter 4 Georgia History 23

Chapter 5 Georgia Business 31

Chapter 6 Seeing the Sights 35

Georgia Time Line 40

Famous Georgians 42

Words to Know 44

To Learn More 45

Useful Addresses 46

Internet Sites 47

Index 48

Fast Facts about Georgia

State Flag

Location: In the southeastern United States, along the Atlantic Ocean
Size: 59,441 square miles (154,547 square kilometers)

Population: 6,917,140 (1993 United States Census Bureau figures)
Capital: Atlanta
Date admitted to the Union: January 2, 1788; the fourth state

Brown thrasher

4

Cherokee rose

Largest cities:
Atlanta,
Columbus,
Savannah, Macon,
Albany, Roswell,
Athens, Augusta,
Marietta, Valdosta
Nicknames: The
Peach State; The
Empire State of
the South

Live oak

State bird: Brown
thrasher
State flower: Cherokee
rose
State tree: Live oak
State song: "Georgia
on My Mind" by
Stuart Gorrell and
Hoagy Carmichael

5

Chapter 1

News Around the Clock

Atlanta, Georgia, is the world headquarters for Cable News Network (CNN). CNN was the first television network to broadcast news 24 hours a day. The broadcasts reach all parts of the world.

Visitors can tour CNN. They can look into the studios from glass-enclosed walkways. They can watch live news broadcasts. Guides explain how the news is gathered.

Ted Turner started CNN in 1980. He is an Atlanta businessperson. CNN is part of the

Visitors can tour the world headquarters of CNN.

Turner Broadcasting System (TBS). TBS also includes the Cartoon Network, Headline News, and Superstation WTBS. In addition, Turner owns the rights to many films, including *Gone with the Wind* and *The Wizard of Oz*.

Land of Peaches

One of Georgia's nicknames is "The Peach State." The state is a leading grower of peaches. Georgia even has a Peach County.

Another nickname for Georgia is "The Empire State of the South." That is because Georgia is the largest southern state. It is also the South's leading producer of goods.

Georgia has many famous landmarks. Savannah was Georgia's first city. Visitors enjoy its many beautiful old homes. One of them belonged to Juliette Low. She founded the Girl Scouts in 1912.

Georgia's capital is Atlanta. Coca-Cola was first served in an Atlanta drugstore. This happened on Peachtree Street in 1886. Today, tall glass-and-steel buildings stand along Peachtree Street.

People enjoy visiting Savannah's beautiful old homes.

Chapter 2

The Land

Georgia is the largest state east of the Mississippi River. Georgia is part of the Deep South. It lies in the southeastern United States.

Georgia is surrounded by five other southern states. North Carolina and Tennessee lie to the north. Alabama is to the west. Florida lies to the south. South Carolina is to the east.

The Atlantic Ocean also touches Georgia's eastern border. Georgia's lowest point is at sea level along the ocean.

Georgia has many kinds of land. Swamps dot the southern plains. Rolling hills lie inland. Mountains stand in northern Georgia.

Swamps dot Georgia's southern plains.

Waterfalls form along southern Georgia's fall line.

Northern Mountains

The Appalachian Mountains run across
northern Georgia. In the northwest, narrow
ridges rise above flat valleys. The soil there is
poor for farming. Wide valleys are to the east.
Crops and cattle are raised there.

The Blue Ridge Mountains stand in
northeastern Georgia. They are part of the
Appalachians. The state's highest point is

there. This is Brasstown Bald Mountain. It rises 4,784 feet (1,435 meters) above sea level.

Hardwood trees and pines cover the Blue Ridge Mountains. The Savannah River begins there. This river forms Georgia's border with South Carolina.

The Piedmont

The Piedmont covers the middle of Georgia. Piedmont means "foot of the mountain." Rolling red hills cover the Piedmont. Red clay gives the ground its color.

Most of Georgia's largest cities are on the Piedmont. The state capital of Atlanta lies on the Chattahoochee River. Marietta and Roswell are nearby. Athens is to the east.

Farther south is the fall line. There, the hills drop to flat, sandy plains. Rivers tumble over falls at this line. The waterfalls provide power. Columbus, Macon, and Augusta are cities on the fall line.

The Coastal Plains

The Coastal Plains are flat. The Gulf Coastal Plain covers southwestern Georgia. The Atlantic

Coastal Plain covers southeastern Georgia. Crops grow well on both plains.

The Okefenokee Swamp covers part of both plains. Cypress trees grow there.

Many islands lie off the Atlantic Coast. Ossabaw, Sapelo, and Cumberland are a few of them.

Wildlife

Bears, foxes, deer, and raccoons roam the Appalachians. Wild turkeys live on the Piedmont. The Okefenokee Swamp is home to alligators and herons. Many kinds of snakes also live in the swamp.

Bass and catfish swim in Georgia's lakes and rivers. Crabs, oysters, and shrimp are found off the coast.

Climate

Georgia has hot, humid summers. Humid means the air is heavy with moisture. Georgia's winters are mild. The Appalachians are cooler than the rest of the state.

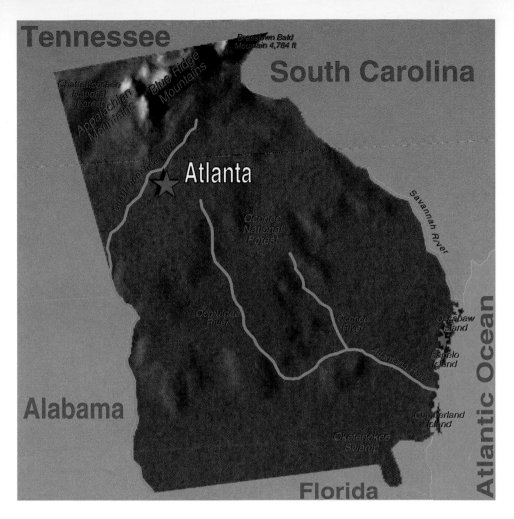

Along the coast, breezes blow in from the Atlantic. Hurricanes sometimes hit the state. A hurricane is a strong windstorm that forms over the ocean. Hurricanes can cause heavy damage when they reach land.

Chapter 3
The People

Georgia has the 11th largest population of the 50 states. It has the fastest-growing population east of the Mississippi.

Many of Georgia's people come from northern states. Some of them take jobs in Georgia's new companies. Other northerners retire in Georgia.

European Backgrounds

More than 70 percent of Georgians have European backgrounds. English, German, and Scottish people settled Georgia's first colonies. A colony is a group of people who settle in a

Many people moved to Georgia to work in its companies.

Georgia's first African people were slaves. They worked on Georgia's plantations.

distant land but remain governed by their native country. The colonists built towns and farmed on the Coastal Plain. Later, Irish, Greek, and Portuguese people came to settle in Georgia.

Today, Georgians celebrate their European backgrounds. Scottish Highland Games are held throughout Georgia. Savannah celebrates St. Patrick's Day for a week. This Irish holiday takes place on March 17.

African Americans

The first Africans came to Georgia in about 1750. They were slaves. Georgia's colonists had started large farms called plantations. The slaves worked on the plantations. They raised rice, tobacco, and indigo. Indigo is a plant used to make blue dye.

By 1860, slaves made up almost 40 percent of Georgia's population. Another 3,500 free African Americans also lived in Georgia.

After the Civil War (1861-1865), all slaves were freed. But African Americans still were not treated equal to whites. Georgia passed laws that kept the races apart. African Americans did not have the right to vote in Georgia.

From the 1920s to the 1970s, many African Americans left Georgia. They headed north and looked for work. Now, thousands are moving back to Georgia. New laws protect the rights of African Americans. Today, about 27 percent of Georgians are African American.

The Gullah People

The Gullah (Guh-LAY) people are African Americans. They live on the Sea Islands. Their ancestors once worked on the islands as slaves.

These people speak the Gullah language. It blends English and West African languages. The Gullah language is heard on Sapelo Island.

The Gullah make their living from farming and fishing. They also make baskets from island grasses.

Native Americans

About 13,000 Native Americans live in Georgia. Most of them are Cherokees and Creeks. Early Cherokees had a written language. They even printed a newspaper called *Cherokee Phoenix*.

Native Americans were forced from Georgia in the early 1800s. Some Cherokees refused to leave. They hid in Georgia's mountains.

Today, their descendants live near Dahlonega. Many Creeks live in southwestern Georgia. Georgia does not have any Indian reservations. A reservation is land set aside for use by Native Americans.

Other Ethnic Groups

Georgia has two other ethnic groups. An ethnic group is people with a common culture. Hispanic Americans make up about 1.5 percent of Georgia's population. This group includes Spanish-speaking people from Mexico, Puerto Rico, and Cuba.

Some Cherokee refused to leave Georgia in the early 1800s. They hid in the mountains.

Some Mexicans are migrant workers. Migrant workers are people who travel from their homes to do seasonal work. They help harvest Georgia's fruit, vegetable, and tobacco crops.

Only about 1 percent of Georgians are Asian Americans. Most of their families came from India, Korea, China, and Vietnam.

Augusta has Georgia's oldest Chinese neighborhood. In 1875, Chinese workers helped build a canal there.

Chapter 4

Georgia History

Georgia's first people arrived about 10,000 years ago. They built huge earthen mounds. Some of these mounds are still standing today.

Later, Cherokee people settled in northern Georgia. Creek people lived in the south.

Spanish Explorers

Hernando de Soto was a Spanish explorer. He was the first European to explore Georgia in 1540. De Soto was looking for gold.

Later, other Spaniards came. They did not settle in Georgia, however.

Georgia's first people built huge earthen mounds. Some of these mounds are still standing today.

English Colonists

By the 1660s, England had 12 colonies. They were north of Georgia along the Atlantic Ocean.

In 1732, King George II added a 13th colony. He gave James Oglethorpe power to found a 13th colony. Oglethorpe brought English colonists to Georgia in 1733.

Oglethorpe named the new colony Georgia after the king.He founded Savannah. This was Georgia's first permanent English town.

The Revolutionary War

In the 1760s, England began taxing the colonists. The colonists thought the taxes were unfair. They started the Revolutionary War (1775-1783). In 1776, they declared their independence from England.

English troops captured Savannah in 1778. Four years later, the colonists drove the English from Georgia. In 1783, the war ended. The United States was a free country.

Leaders of the new country wrote a constitution. On January 2, 1788, Georgia approved the United States Constitution.

Savannah was Georgia's first permanent English town.

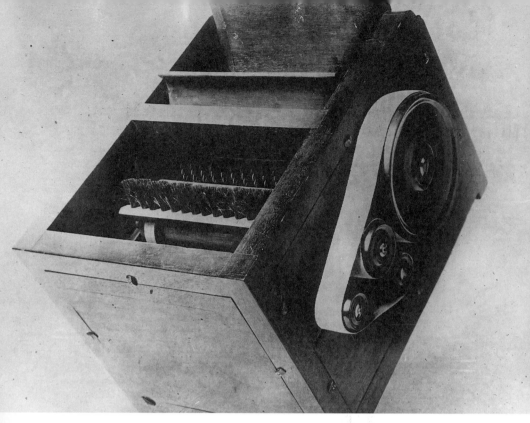

Eli Whitney invented the cotton gin in 1792.

Georgia became the fourth state to join the Union. Augusta became the state capital.

The Civil War

In 1792, Eli Whitney invented the cotton gin in Georgia. This machine cleaned the seeds from the cotton. It allowed plantation owners to plant and harvest more cotton. Georgia became a major cotton-growing state. Owners needed even more slaves to work the fields.

Many people in the North were against slavery. In 1860, Abraham Lincoln was elected president of the United States. He was a Northerner. Southerners feared that Lincoln would ban slavery.

Georgia and 10 southern states left the Union. They formed the Confederacy. In 1861, the Civil War started. The Confederacy won a great battle in Georgia. It was at Chickamauga Creek in 1863.

In 1864, Union General William Tecumseh Sherman invaded northern Georgia. His troops burned Atlanta. Sherman's troops then marched from Atlanta to Savannah. They destroyed everything in their path.

The South surrendered in 1865. The Union freed all the slaves. Georgia was in ruins.

Reconstruction

Georgia underwent Reconstruction. This means Georgia reorganized and reestablished itself. Georgia's leaders had to change its laws. They rewrote the state constitution. African Americans were given the right to vote. In 1870, Georgia was readmitted to the Union.

Georgians also rebuilt their railroads, cities, factories, and farms. The capital was moved from Augusta to Atlanta in 1868.

In the 1920s, boll weevils destroyed Georgia's cotton crop.

Boll Weevils, Depression, and War

Cotton was still Georgia's most important crop. In the 1920s, beetles called boll weevils destroyed Georgia's cotton plants. Many farmers lost their farms.

Some farmers started growing other crops. Peaches, pecans, and peanuts became important.

Then the Great Depression (1929-1939) hit the United States. Factories closed. Many

Georgians lost their jobs. Prices for crops dropped. Georgia farmers were pushed from their land.

The U.S. government wanted to help people. So it hired Georgians to build housing and roads.

In 1941, the United States entered World War II (1939-1945). Georgia built planes and ships for the war effort.

After the war, many northern businesses moved to Georgia. They could pay lower wages there.

Recent Changes

Georgians are working hard for better schools. In 1985, Georgia passed the Quality Basic Education Act. It developed programs designed to help children do better in school. In 1993, Georgia started a state lottery. Lottery money is used for education.

New companies continue to come to Georgia. More than 1,000 of them are high-tech companies. High-tech means advanced technology, especially in electronics and computers.

In July 1996, Atlanta hosted the Olympic Games. Thousands of people from around the world came to the city.

Chapter 5

Georgia Business

Georgia has a strong economy. Service industries, manufacturing, and farming are Georgia's most important businesses.

Service Industries

Trade is Georgia's biggest service industry. Some people in trade sell goods from factories to stores.

Georgia earns about $11 billion a year from tourism. Visitors spend this money at Georgia's restaurants, resorts, and hotels.

People in real estate sell land, homes, and office buildings. Thousands of new homes have been built near Atlanta. Factories and office buildings have gone up throughout the state.

Georgia earns about $11 billion a year from tourism.

Coca-Cola's world headquarters is in Atlanta, Georgia.

Agriculture and Fishing

Georgia leads the nation in growing peanuts and pecans. Peaches are another leading crop. Cotton, tobacco, and sweet potatoes are important, too.

Broiler chickens are Georgia's leading farm product. Broilers are five- to 12-week-old chickens. Most broilers and eggs come from northeastern Georgia.

Georgia's fishing business makes about $20 million a year. Shrimp and crab are the most important catches.

Manufacturing

Textiles are Georgia's leading manufactured goods. Textiles include carpet, cloth, and yarn. Dalton makes more carpet than any other U.S. city.

Food is Georgia's second-leading manufactured good. Workers make peanut butter from Georgia peanuts. Broilers become packaged chicken. Soft drinks are another product. The world headquarters for Coca-Cola is in Atlanta.

Georgia factories also make cars and airplanes. Marietta is home to Lockheed. This company designs and builds aircraft.

Companies make toilet paper and cardboard. The materials come from Georgia's trees. Georgia-Pacific is a well-known paper company.

Mining

Georgia leads the nation in mining clay and granite. A huge belt of kaolin clay lies across central Georgia. It is used in making china dishes. Granite used in construction is found in northeastern Georgia.

Chapter 6

Seeing the Sights

Visitors have much to see and do in Georgia. They can hike in the mountains. They can watch animals in wildlife refuges. They can visit Georgia's historical sites.

Northern Georgia

Chickamauga Battlefield lies in Georgia's northwestern corner. The visitor center shows many kinds of guns and cannons that were used during the Civil War.

The Appalachian Trail is in north central Georgia. It begins in Georgia's Blue Ridge Mountains. It ends in Maine. Hikers try to walk the 2,144-mile (3,430-kilometer) route.

At Chickamauga Battlefield, people can see the kinds of guns and cannons that were used during the Civil War.

35

Dahlonega is just south of the Appalachian Trail. The first gold rush in the United States happened there in 1828. Today, visitors can pan for gold at Crisson's Gold Mine.

Calhoun is west of Dahlonega. Near Calhoun is New Echota State Historic Site. This was the last capital of the Cherokee nation. The printing office of the *Cherokee Phoenix* has been rebuilt there.

Around Atlanta

Atlanta lies on the Piedmont. Atlanta is Georgia's largest city. It is also the state capital.

The spot where Atlanta first started now lies underground. Underground Atlanta has shops and restaurants. They lie beneath the streets. Many storefronts are from the 1800s.

Nearby and above ground is the World of Coca-Cola. This museum shows the history of the famous soft drink.

The Martin Luther King Jr. National Historic District is across town. King was a great African-American leader. His church and birthplace are open to the public.

Atlanta University Center has the largest concentration of African-American schools in the United States.

Six Flags Over Georgia is west of Atlanta. It is an amusement park. Riders scream on its Georgia Cyclone roller coaster.

East of Atlanta is Stone Mountain Park. Stone Mountain has the world's largest piece of exposed granite. A huge sculpture is carved into the granite. It shows three heroes of the Confederacy. They are Robert E. Lee, Stonewall Jackson, and Jefferson Davis.

Other Piedmont Cities

Athens lies east of Atlanta. The University of Georgia is there, where about 28,000 students attend classes.

Augusta is southeast of Athens. Pro golfers play at Augusta National Golf Course. The Masters Golf Tournament is held there each April.

Macon is in the middle of Georgia. More than 200,000 cherry trees grow in Macon. Each March, Macon holds the Cherry Blossom Festival.

Columbus is on Georgia's eastern border. Fort Benning is outside of town. This is the world's largest infantry training base. Infantry means soldiers who fight on foot. The Infantry Museum is on the base. It shows the history of the American foot soldier.

Southern Georgia

Andersonville is southeast of Columbus. The Southern soldiers built a prison there. It held about 33,000 Union soldiers. Almost 13,000 died because of the bad conditions. Today, visitors can see some buildings and escape tunnels.

The tiny town of Plains is south of Andersonville. This is former President Jimmy Carter's hometown. He still lives there.

Okefenokee National Wildlife Refuge is in the southeast corner. Tour boats take visitors through the swamp's waterways. A trail winds past cypress trees, swamp grass, and alligators.

The Atlantic Coast

Off the southern coast lies Cumberland Island National Seashore. Wild pigs, turkeys, and deer live on the island.

Savannah is north along the coast. This was Georgia's first city. Savannah has many beautiful old homes.

The First African Baptist Church also stands in Savannah. It dates from 1773. This is the oldest African-American church in the country.

Ships of the Sea Museum is on the Savannah River. It displays models of many seagoing craft. Visitors learn about the sailing life there.

Georgia Time Line

8000 B.C.—Early people build huge mounds.

A.D. 1000—Cherokee and Creek people begin settling in Georgia.

1540—Hernando de Soto explores Georgia for Spain.

1733—James Oglethorpe lands with the first colonists; Savannah is founded.

1742—Oglethorpe defeats the Spanish at the Battle of Bloody Marsh.

1775-1783—Georgia helps the 13 colonies win independence from England.

1788—Georgia becomes the fourth state.

1828—Cherokee Indians at New Echota print the *Cherokee Phoenix*, the first Native American newspaper.

1838—The Cherokee are forced from Georgia.

1861—Georgia secedes from the Union and joins the Confederacy; the Civil War begins.

1864—Union General Sherman burns Atlanta.

1870—Georgia is readmitted to the Union.

1886—John Pemberton invents Coca-Cola in Atlanta.

1912—Juliette Low establishes the Girl Scouts of America at Savannah.

1920s—Boll weevils destroy Georgia's cotton crops.

1943—Georgia is the first state to allow 18-year-olds to vote.

1945—President Franklin D. Roosevelt dies at Warm Springs, Georgia.

1961—African Americans are admitted to the University of Georgia.

1973—Maynard Jackson Jr. is elected mayor of Atlanta and becomes the first African-American mayor of a large southern city.

1976—Jimmy Carter from Plains, Georgia, is elected president of the United States.

1983—A Marietta team wins the Little League World Series.

1994—The Super Bowl football game is played in Atlanta.

1996—Atlanta hosts the Summer Olympics.

Famous Georgians

Kim Basinger (1953-) Actress who bought the town of Braselton for making movies; born in Athens.

Jimmy Carter (1924-) Peanut farmer and naval officer who became president of the United States (1977-1981); born in Plains.

Ty Cobb (1886-1961) Baseball slugger who hit for an all-time record average of .367; elected to the Baseball Hall of Fame in 1936; born in Banks City.

Newt Gingrich (1943-) History professor and politician who served Georgia in the U.S. House of Representatives (1979-) and became the Speaker of the House of Representatives in 1995; lives in Marietta.

Oliver Hardy (1892-1957) Comedy film star; part of the Laurel and Hardy team; born in Atlanta.

Martin Luther King Jr. (1929-1968) Baptist minister and civil-rights leader who won the Nobel Peace Prize in 1964; born in Atlanta.

Gladys Knight (1946-) Singer who formed a group called the Pips; winner of four Grammy Awards; born in Atlanta.

Juliette Low (1860-1927) Founded the Girl Scouts of America in 1912; born in Savannah.

"Little Richard" Penniman (1932-) Rock-and-roll singer and pianist whose songs include "Tutti Frutti"; born in Macon.

Cynthia McKinney (1955-) Professor and politican who became the first African-American woman to serve from Georgia in the U.S. House of Representatives (1993-).

Jackie Robinson (1919-1972) Baseball player who became the first African American to play in the major leagues; born in Cairo.

Sequoya (1760-1843) Cherokee scholar who invented the first alphabet for a Native American language; lived in New Echota.

Ted Turner (1938-) Businessperson who developed CNN in Atlanta; owner of the Atlanta Braves and the Atlanta Hawks.

Alice Walker (1944-) Author and poet who won the Pulitzer Prize in fiction for *The Color Purple*; born in Eatonton.

Trisha Yearwood (1964-) Country-western singer; born in Monticello.

Words to Know

boll weevil—a beetle that destroys cotton seeds and fiber

colony—a group of people who settle in a distant land but remain governed by their native country

cotton gin—a device that separates cotton seeds from cotton fiber

ethnic group—people with a common culture

high tech—a short way of saying high technology, which is the making of computers and electronic parts

humid—air that is heavy with moisture

hurricane—a strong windstorm that forms over an ocean and causes great damage when it reaches land

infantry—soldiers who fight on foot

migrant—a person who moves to do seasonal work

plantation—a large farm that usually grows one main crop

population—the number of people in a place

reservation—land set aside for use by Native Americans

textile—yarn, thread, and cloth

tourism—the business of providing services such as food and lodging for travelers

To Learn More

Fradin, Dennis B. *Georgia*. From Sea to Shining Sea. Chicago: Children's Press, 1991.

Kent, Zachary A. *Georgia*. America the Beautiful. Chicago: Children's Press, 1988.

LaDoux, Rita C. *Georgia*. Hello USA. Minneapolis: Lerner Publications, 1991.

Pederson, Anne. *Kidding Around Atlanta*. Santa Fe, N.M.: John Muir Publications, 1989.

Snow, Pegeen. *Atlanta*. A Downtown America Book. New York: Dillon Press, 1988.

Useful Addresses

CNN Studio Tour
1 CNN Center
P.O. Box 105366
Atlanta, GA 30348-5366

Chattahoochee River National Recreation Area
1978 Island Ford Parkway
Dunwoody, GA 30350

Dahlonega Gold Museum Historic Site
Public Square
Box 2042
Dahlonega, GA 30533

Martin Luther King Jr. National Historic Site
522 Auburn Avenue NE
Atlanta, GA 30312

Ships of the Sea Maritime Museum
503 East River Street
Savannah, GA 31401

Stone Mountain Park
Box 778
Stone Mountain, GA 30086

Internet Sites

City.Net Georgia
http://city.net/countries/united_states/georgia

Travel.org—Georgia
http://travel.org/georgia.html

State of Georgia Home Page
http://www.state.ga.us

CNN Studio Tour
http://www.cnn.com/StudioTour/
StudioTour1.html

Index

Appalachian Mountains, 12, 14

Appalachian Trail, 35-36

Atlanta, 4-5, 7, 9, 13, 27, 31, 33, 36-37

Atlantic Ocean, 4, 11, 15

Augusta, 5, 13, 26-27, 37

Blue Ridge Mountains, 12-13, 35

Chattahoochee River, 13

Cherokee Phoenix, 20, 36

Cherry Blossom Festival, 37

CNN, 7

coastal plains, 13-14, 18

Coca-Cola, 9, 33

cotton, 26, 28, 32

De Soto, Hernando, 23

fall line, 13

First African Baptist Church, 39

Gullah, 19-20

indigo, 19

kaolin clay, 33

King, Martin Luther Jr., 36

Lincoln, Abraham, 27

Macon, 5, 13, 37

Masters Golf Tournament, 37

migrant, 21

Oglethorpe, James, 24

Okefenokee Swamp, 14, 38

Olympic Games, 29

peach, 5, 9, 28, 32

Piedmont, 13

Quality Basic Education Act, 29

Savannah, 5, 9, 18, 24, 27, 39

Sherman, William Tecumseh, 27

Turner, Ted, 7

Whitney, Eli, 26